Help My Unbelief

BARNABAS PIPER

LifeWay Press®
Nashville, Tennessee

Editorial Team

Reid Patton
Content Editor

Susan Hill
Production Editor

Jon Rodda
Art Director

Joel Polk
Editorial Team Leader

Brian Daniel
Manager,Short-Term Disicpleship

Michael Kelley
Director, Discipleship and Groups Ministry

Ben Mandrell
President, LifeWay Christian Resources

Published by LifeWay Press® • © 2020 Barnabas Piper

ISBN 978-1-5359-6236-0• Item 005816357

Deweydecimalclassification:234.2
Subject Headings:: FAITH / BELIEF AND DOUBT / GOD

Unless otherwise indicated, all Scripture quotations are from Scripture quotations are from the ESV® Bible (The Holy Bible, English Standard Version®), copyright © 2001 by Crossway, a publishing ministry of Good News Publishers. Used by permission. Allrights reserved.

Scripture quotations marked CSB have been taken from the Christian Standard Bible®, Copyright © 2017 by Holman Bible Publishers. Used by permission. Christian Standard Bible® and CSB® are federally registered trademarks of Holman Bible Publishers.

Photography Credits
Cover and page 98: Rieserferner-Ahrn Nature Park, Italy. Eberhard Grossgasteiger/Unsplash
Pages 8, 12, 24, 39: Judean Desert, Israel. Jon Rodda
Pages 40, 51: Big Horn County, Wyoming. Jon Rodda
Pages 54, 65: The Needles, Custer State Park, South Dakota. Jon Rodda
Pages 68, 72: Jenny Lake, Grand Teton National Park, Wyoming. Jon Rodda
Pages 85, 93: Kepler Cascades, Yellowstone National Park, Wyoming. Jon Rodda

To order additional copies of this resource, write to LifeWay Resources Customer Service; One LifeWay Plaza; Nashville, TN 37234; fax 615-251-5933; call toll free 800-458-2772; order online at LifeWay.com; or email orderentry@lifeway.com.

Printed in the United States of America

Groups Ministry Publishing • LifeWay Resources • One LifeWay Plaza • Nashville, TN 37234

Contents

About the Author

BARNABAS PIPER is the author of three books: *The Pastors Kid, Help My Unbelief*, and *The Curious Christian*. He cohosts two podcasts, *The Happy Rant* and *The Table of (mal)Contents*, writes for *He Reads Truth*, and has contributed to numerous other websites and publications. Piper speaks regularly at churches and conferences around the country and lives in Nashville with his two daughters and serves on staff at his church, Immanuel Nashville.

Introduction

Every Christian doubts. If you haven't yet, give it a minute—you will.

I spent my first thirty years as a pastor's kid. I knew my Bible inside and out. I was the Sunday school answer man, helped lead youth group worship, and generally looked the part of a good Christian boy. I have believed the truths of Christianity nearly all my life. I have believed in Jesus as my Savior, in the Trinity, in the inspired and infallible Word of God. And yet ...

> ... I have committed sins that have deeply wounded others and nearly destroyed my relationship with Jesus.

> ... I have regularly decided my way is better than God's.

> ... I doubt God's promises.

> ... I'm skeptical. I know what Scripture says, I know the arguments, but the questions nag at me.

> ... I struggle to even know what belief means.

Maybe you share my doubts, or maybe you have your own. Or maybe you have never doubted Scripture or God because you're afraid of mystery or have simply never given it much thought.

Whichever place you're coming from, I'm so glad you're participating in this study. We'll ask big questions about the nature of doubt and belief, and we'll explore how Jesus responded to doubters. We'll look at what kinds of questions build faith and which kind destroy it. And we'll reflect on who God is as the object of faith and how He gives faith to doubters.

So bring your belief, strong or weak. Bring your questions, big or small. Let's take them before the Lord and see what true faith looks like. There's no better place to take our questions.

How to Use This Study

This Bible-study book includes six weeks
of content for group and personal study.

Group Sessions

Regardless of what day of the week your group meets, each week of content begins with the group session. Each group session uses the following format to facilitate simple yet meaningful interaction among group members, with God's Word, and with the video teaching from author Barnabas Piper

START. This page includes questions to get the conversation started and to introduce the video teaching.

WATCH. This page provides space to take notes on the video teaching.

DISCUSS. This page includes questions and statements that guide the group to respond to Barnabas's teaching and to explore relevant biblical truth.

Personal Study

Each week provides three days of Bible study and learning activities for individual engagement between group sessions. The personal study revisits stories, Scriptures, and themes introduced in the video teaching, so that participants can understand and apply them on a personal level.

Each personal study includes the following three sections:

Know   Be   Do

Digital Resources

EBOOK. In addition to the print book, this book is also available as an ebook, which is immediately available after purchase in your LifeWay Reader library.

ENHANCED EBOOK. In addition to the ebook, an enhanced ebook featuring integrated video assets such as a promotional video and session previews is also available after purchase in your LifeWay Reader library.

VIDEO SESSIONS. All 6 video teaching sessions are available to rent or purchase as individual, downloadable sessions. Additionally, you'll find a group use bundle that gives your church a license to share digital video content with multiple groups in your church.

For these resources and more, visit LifeWay.com/HelpMyUnbelief.

Week 1

Where Doubt Comes From

Start

Welcome to Session 1.

When many of us hear the word "doubt," we think it's sinful. To question God is wrong, right? Well, that depends on the definition of doubt. We need to know what, "doubt" is before we can begin to figure out how to deal with it.

How would you define "doubt"?

Give an example of a doubt you've had before?

In this session, we're going to answer the big question, "What is doubt?" To understand doubt, we have to understand who God is, since He's the one we're doubting, and we have to understand ourselves in relationship to Him. We're going to face some big, foundational biblical truths—about who God is and who we are as Created beings—and see how those truths relate to our doubts.

**ASK SOMEONE TO PRAY THEN WATCH
THE VIDEO TEACHING FOR SESSION 1.**

Watch

Use this page to take notes during the video teaching.

Discuss

USE THE FOLLOWING QUESTIONS TO FACILITATE YOUR GROUP DISCUSSION.

Doubt is a profoundly personal, deeply felt struggle for many people. In the coming sessions, we'll engage that side of it, but in this session we explore the big questions of doubt: what is it, and where does it come from? These are big idea questions and will lay an important foundation for understanding God, doubt, and faith that moves us forward.

This session defined doubt, in it's most basic form, as "simply not knowing." Why, then, is doubt not necessarily sinful?

What do our doubts say about us?

What do our doubts say about God?

Read Psalm 139:6. If God is infinite and we're not, why are many of our doubts natural?

What stirs up your doubts?

How do you respond when you doubt? Do you feel guilty when you doubt? Why or why not?

How has today's session changed the way you think about your doubts?

CLOSE THE GROUP IN PRAYER. REMIND THE GROUP TO COMPLETE THE THREE PERSONAL STUDIES BEFORE THE NEXT MEETING.

Scripture sets up a relationship between God and man that shows His infinity and our limitations.

Know

Personal Study 1

READ GENESIS 1.

What does this passage tell us about the relationship between God and people?

How should we think about God as a result?

From its very first words, Scripture sets up a relationship between God and man that shows His infinity and our limitations. He's the Creator, and we're the created. He existed before time began, and we exist within time. He's eternal, and we have a life span. He always has been, and we came into existence at a specific time, and our bodies will pass away at a specific time. He created everything from nothing, and we're part of that, spoken into existence with words.

To understand God, and our own doubts, it's vital that we grasp this relationship. We tend to go through life with the assumption that we can learn, discover, and comprehend anything if we truly want to. We see ourselves as the masters of our domain with the world at our fingertips. We have technology, science, and cultural advancements on our side. We build lives of ease and efficiency with the aim of security and comfort. And we rarely, if ever, consider our limitations or God's lack of them.

Think about your own life and relationship with God. What does it mean for you that God is infinitely good, wise, and powerful?

How difficult is it for you to acknowledge your limitations? Why is humility an important aspect of our faith-walks?

God created all that exists, so He stands outside of and beyond the created order. God was, is, and will be forever. God spoke all things into existence and created our ability to learn, create, think, solve, build, and make. Despite all our efforts, we'll reach the end of our abilities. We'll max out our understanding. We live within a defined time frame and a limited capacity for understanding. Refusing to acknowledge these limitations only leads to hurt, sorrow, and confusion.

READ GENESIS 3.

Where do we see doubt in this passage?

In Genesis 3, Satan tempted Adam and Eve to doubt the goodness of God. They foolishly chose to pursue being gods rather than trusting what God said. They wanted God's knowledge for themselves. They wanted His deity and infinity, so they broke His explicit command. In doing so, they introduced sin into the world, and they doomed themselves and every person to follow to death. In one bittersweet bite of fruit, the world went from paradise to graveyard. Adam and Eve's doubts led them away from God.

In what areas of life are you most tempted to doubt God?

The consequence of sin was a curse. It's not a spell or a fairy tale curse that can be broken by a kiss or a quest. It isn't limited to a person or place. It's pervasive, touching every person everywhere for every moment of all time. The curse taints every aspect of life: relational, physical, spiritual, emotional, and intellectual.

This means that every thought we have, every discovery, advancement, and invention—they're all flawed and incomplete. And it means that our view of ourselves is broken too.

Think about the curse that God institutes in Genesis 3 (vv. 14–19). How does the curse affect how we relate to other people? How we work? How we view ourselves?

We want knowledge, like God. We want to be gods of our own lives, and we often don't even realize these sinful impulses. The fall has blinded us and we can't see what is true as reality. We love things we shouldn't, believe things we shouldn't, and are skeptical of things that are true and good.

When we consider God's perfect holiness, the curse becomes that much bleaker. Before, we were limited in our understanding of God by being finite. Now we're sinful, blind, self-worshipping, and further removed from a true understanding of God.

How does the curse impact our ability to understand and see God for who He is? How does it shape how we view ourselves in relationship to Him?

We've seen two significant realities that shape how we see and understand God. First, God is infinite, and we're finite. Second, God is perfect, and we're sinful. It seems obvious, then, that we would struggle to understand God. With our limitations and weaknesses and His infinity and holiness, we're bound to reach the borders of our understanding. We don't have the capacity to fully understand an infinite God.

Now we're at the core of where doubt comes from. Doubt, in its most basic form, is when we say, "I don't know." It's simply being unsure. Doubt happens when we don't understand. For finite, sinful people like us, of course, we'll experience doubts about God.

Why are we so uncomfortable admitting "I don't know" when it comes to God?

God is constantly thinking and doing things at a level beyond our comprehension. At every moment, God is sustaining the entire universe, knowing every thought, weaving every life, and working His perfect plan for all creation. He never stops. We can't possibly comprehend even a minuscule fraction of God's perfect knowledge and wisdom. We shouldn't be expected to fully understand God.

As you reflect on these truths, something should stir in your mind; doubt isn't necessarily a sin. To doubt is human; it's natural. It's a direct result of being who we are—finite creatures seeking to understand things beyond ourselves. We'll inevitably doubt. It's inevitable we'll question, wonder, and be unsure.

Scripture is full of people with questions and doubts. Gideon asked God for a sign because he was afraid (Judges 6:36–40). Hannah pleaded with God for a son with the kind of pain that only comes from fear and doubt (1 Sam. 1:1–11). Job lost everything and wondered aloud why such a thing would happen (Job 3:11). The Psalms overflow with prayers asking where God is, when He'll return, has He forgotten his people, and more. The prophets lamented and mourned and wondered when God would rescue His people. Thomas didn't know how to believe in Jesus' resurrection until he saw Him in the flesh (John 20:25).

Why did the writers of Scripture include stories about people of faith who wrestled with questions and doubts?

How does knowing that people of faith struggled with doubt change your definition of what it means to be a mature Christian?

To doubt is human. It's how we respond when we doubt that determines whether or not it's a sin. You can doubt in a way that draws you closer to faith in God, or you can doubt in a way that undermines and dissolves your faith. We'll study this distinction further in the coming sessions.

Since doubting is human and normal, what is it that separates sinful doubt from the kind that builds our faith?

What kind of response to doubt should we have in order to strengthen our faith in God?

Be

Personal Study 2

We saw in the first study that in one sense, doubt is not knowing. It comes from our limitations and sinfulness, an inability to see and understand all that God is, and all that He is doing. It's innate to humans to simply not know, to misunderstand, and to, therefore, doubt.

On the other hand, that's not where it feels like doubt comes from much of the time. For some of us, doubt is intellectual—big questions about God and deep questions about reality or truth. For many others, though, doubt is experiential. It wells up when circumstances aren't right, and life is hard; death, illness, unemployment, divorce, financial hardship, broken relationships, betrayals, tragedies, natural disasters. The pain and loss we feel stirs up questions we cannot answer, most notably and consistently, "WHY?"

This study will not likely answer that question (sorry!), but hopefully, it will help you know what to do with it. Because that really matters. How you ask questions in the midst of hardship and to whom you ask them could be the difference between drawing closer to God or leaving the faith.

When you think about times you've asked "why?" in difficult circumstances, where have you gone for answers? Has that been helpful? Why or why not?

Do your doubts stem more from intellectual questions or experiential hardship? What motivates you to look for answers?

Intellectual questions   **Experiential doubt**

Let's look at a passage that can help us consider our doubts and struggles and give us some clarity and comfort.

Psalm 139:1-6 says:

> *Lord, you have searched me and known me.*
> *You know when I sit down and when I stand up;*
> *you understand my thoughts from far away.*
> *You observe my travels and my rest;*
> *you are aware of all my ways.*
> *Before a word is on my tongue,*
> *you know all about it, Lord.*
> *You have encircled me;*
> *you have placed your hand on me.*
> *This wondrous knowledge is beyond me.*
> *It is lofty; I am unable to reach it.*
> **PSALM 139:1-6**

Verses 1–5 should comfort us with the reality that God cares for us and is always with us. Everything described in verses 1–5, everything we find comforting, stems from the bigness of God and His constant awareness, foreknowledge, power, and protection at all times. These characterestics demonstrate the sovereignty and infinity of God. They are expressions of God's power and character on behalf of His people.

What does this passage reveal about God's character?

How does possessing an understanding of God's character help us trust Him even when we don't have all the answers?

In verse 6, the passage culminates in wonder. David wrote that the ways and wisdom of God are too wondrous to be understood by mere humans. This is primarily a statement of worship. The very things about God that cause us to doubt—those aspects of His character that are infinite and mysterious—are the very reason we can trust Him in faith.

Psalm 139 offers a gentle but non-ignorable answer: it's not always for us to know, but we can always trust. This doesn't mean it's wrong to ask why, to wonder, or to feel the deep ache of why. It does mean that it's wrong for us to resent or mistrust God when there isn't a readily apparent answer.

How does knowing that some things are beyond our grasp actually help with our doubts?

Our knee jerk reaction is to think "that doesn't make sense" or "that isn't right." But to think like this is to make the tacit assumption that we know better than God and to assume that our instincts are more correct than His Word. When the Scripture declares God's knowledge "too wondrous," it gives context to our questions and doubts—they're real, they're powerful, they matter, and they exist inside the infinite wisdom and goodness of God. The moment our questions and doubts move us to a place of thinking God's Word isn't right and we know best is when our doubts have become sin.

Why is it so natural for us to think that our understanding is greater than God's?

What level of trust do you place on the Word of God? How do you reconcile your opinions and feelings with the Word of God? What or who is the final authority in your life?

Your questions aren't too big for God. God is immense while also being close, personal, caring, and attentive (Ps. 139:1–5). We must never confuse God's greatness for God being distant. God is love (1 John 4:8) and nothing earthly, spiritual, or circumstantial can separate the children of God from His love (Rom. 8:38-38). We know this because He sent Jesus to be one of us, fully human while maintaining full deity, and to live the life we couldn't live and die the death we deserved to die.

So when we're confronted with "Why?" and see no clear answer, that's OK. God has the answer, and God is not far away. God not only has the answer, God is the answer to all our doubts and questions. He's close, He's watching, and He's caring.

At every moment God is sustaining the entire universe, knowing every thought, weaving every life, and working His perfect plan for all creation.

How can we keep in mind God's greatness and infinity when we begin to doubt and question?

Do

Personal Study 3

We've examined doubt from the outside—where it comes from, the nature of it, and how we should think about it. That kind of study is helpful and necessary. But doubt is also deeply personal and isn't something we should only examine clinically or externally. Let's examine doubt from the inside: how you experience doubt and think about it. Whether you struggle deeply with doubt or not at all, put thought and prayer into these questions. Be honest with yourself and with God as you answer and see what He reveals about Himself, faith, and your heart.

What kinds of doubts have you experienced or struggled with? What questions have nagged at you or scared you enough you've been afraid even to ask?

How have you handled questions about God or Scripture that seem unanswerable, the mysterious or difficult portions of the Bible?

Do you struggle to find peace with the idea
that God knows things and acts in ways beyond
your understanding? Why or why not?

Have you felt guilt for doubting? If so, how has this session
affected those feelings? If not, why do you think that is?

When you doubt, what do you do? How do you respond?

Week 2
Doubts that Break Our Faith

Start

Welcome to Session 2.

**What was one key takeaway from
your personal study last week?**

Last session, the question was posed, "Is doubt sin?" and we came to this conclusion: It's how we respond when we doubt that determines whether it's a sin. You can doubt in a way that draws you closer to faith in God, or you can doubt in a way that undermines and dissolves your faith.

**As you've thought about your own doubts, do
your doubts draw you closer to God or drive
a wedge in your relationship with Him?**

That's the issue we'll address in this session: how we doubt, particularly, how we shouldn't doubt. We'll walk through what it looks like to doubt in such a way our faith is undermined and ruined. We'll explore the kinds of attitudes and beliefs that lead us down this road and examine ways to avoid them without dodging hard questions.

How do we contemplate hard questions, mysteries, and uncertainty without losing our faith? That's the question we are about to answer.

**ASK SOMEONE TO PRAY THEN WATCH
THE VIDEO TEACHING FOR SESSION 2.**

Watch

Use this page to take notes during the video teaching.

Discuss

USE THE FOLLOWING QUESTIONS TO
FACILITATE YOUR GROUP DISCUSSION.

This session explored one side of doubt—the negative side. It looked at what kind of doubt becomes sin. And it left a big question mostly unanswered: How can doubt build our faith? That's OK and on purpose. We'll explore that in the coming sessions, but for this discussion, focus on how you respond to questions and doubts.

Thinking about your own doubts, are you most likely to take questions to God and His Word, or do you look elsewhere?

Have someone read Hebrews 11:1. How does this verse highlight the tension between faith and doubt?

What do you think the difference is between doubts that destroy faith and doubts that build it up?

When you hear the phrase "God says it, I believe it, that settles it" what does it mean to you? How does this phrase dismiss doubts that need to be dealt with?

Can you think of any biblical examples of those who doubted? How did they handle their questions/doubts? What were the results?

What experiences do you have of questions/ doubts drawing you closer to God?

CLOSE THE GROUP IN PRAYER. REMIND THE GROUP TO COMPLETE THE THREE PERSONAL STUDIES BEFORE THE NEXT MEETING.

Know

Personal Study 1

Now faith is the reality of what is hoped
for, the proof of what is not seen.
HEBREWS 11:1 (CSB)

Now faith is the assurance of things hoped
for, the conviction of things not seen.
HEBREWS 11:1 (ESV)

What do you notice about the connection
between doubt and faith in this verse?

In Hebrews 11:1, we see something mind-bending, and looks almost like a contradiction in terms. We see faith defined in terms that seem opposed to one another—reality or assurance of hope, proof, or conviction of the unseen. If something is hoped for and is unseen, that means we're inevitably unsure of it. We may be confident and may believe strongly in it, but we aren't sure. But this verse says faith is the assurance of those things, the conviction of them. Faith proves to our hearts the very thing we're unsure of. Confounding, right?

How has faith given you proof when you
would have otherwise been unsure?

As long as we're wading in deep waters, let's go a little deeper. The further implication in this verse is that faith and doubt are inseparable. If there is no doubt, there can be no faith. Hebrews 11 inextricably links something we don't like and don't think is good (doubt) to something we desperately want and know we need (faith). But if you remember that doubt *is not* inherently sinful and *is* inherently human, this verse becomes clearer.

**Does it make you uncomfortable to link
doubt and faith? Explain.**

Of course, faith and doubt are inseparably linked. How else could we believe anything about an infinite, perfect God? Our instinct is to want clear answers and empirical evidence for every idea. We want neat and tidy truths summed up clearly, but with God we get no such thing. We certainly can't reduce Him to a size we can wrap our heads around. Nor can we overcome our sinful blindness and skewed perspective on our own. Questions will remain unanswered. Evidence will be unsatisfactory. We'll never neatly systematize and sum up God. This means that faith, the assurance and confidence of those things we hope for in the Lord and the conviction of those things we haven't seen about Him, is the only right response to doubt. There can be no faith without doubt.

But there can be doubt without faith. This is the doubt that destroys faith and is what I call "unbelieving doubt."

**Does "unbelieving doubt" sound redundant
to you? What's the alternative?**

When unbelieving doubt poses a question, it's not interested in the answer for any reason other than to disprove it. If you're experiencing this kind of doubt, you're not asking questions to learn; you're asking in order to undermine and don't want to progress to an answer. You want to show that there's no answer or to deflect and disparage the answer, so you don't have to believe it. Unbelieving doubt isn't working toward anything true but merely against belief. These doubts are the wild monsters that wreck faith.

How does a person get here? What separates unbelieving doubt from believing doubt? (I know, "believing doubt" sounds like a contradiction; an explanation is forthcoming).

Ultimately the answer is this: unbelieving doubt is placing your faith in the wrong thing. That's right; unbelieving doubt is based on faith. It may refuse to have faith in God or His Word, but it absolutely functions on faith—faith in self. Doubt that destroys our faith in Jesus is actually faith in ourselves.

What do you think when you read "unbelieving doubt is based on faith"? Faith in what or whom? Can a person go through life with no faith at all?

Resistance to God's Word as true and authoritative communicates that you define truth and are your own authority.

Consider this: a refusal to believe God is an affirmation that I know better; it's the belief that God doesn't know best. Thus, it's a belief in my knowledge, my way, my wisdom. A resistance to seeing God's Word as true and authoritative is an affirmation that I define truth and am my own authority. Unbelieving doubt is an assertion that I am god and is idolatry of me.

Think back to Genesis 3, when Adam and Eve sinned in the garden of Eden and brought sin and death into God's perfect creation. They chose to believe God didn't really know best, that He wasn't telling the truth. Their doubt in God was belief in a lie.

How did Adam and Eve exercise faith in themselves by disbelieving God?

In what areas are you tempted to trust your own judgment over and above what God has said?

It takes faith to doubt God just as much as it does to believe in God. Except that this faith is based on a finite, sinful person who will inevitably follow in the footsteps of Adam and Eve.

The doubt that undermines faith is not a doubt of simply being unsure; we're all unsure at different points in time. Unbelieving doubt is a refusal to believe and a conviction that what I'm unsure of is more sure than what God said. And to hold this conviction, you must believe profoundly in yourself and your ability to know, understand, and outwit God.

Where do you see unbelieving doubt at work in the world around you?

While there are things God says and does that are beyond our comprehension, why is it so easy to forget what He has done and said that we can understand (the exodus, His promises, the cross, the Resurrection, etc.)?

The Bible frequently reminds us to remember God's past faithfulness in order to believe in Him in the present and future. God often says of Himself, "I am the Lord who brought you out of Egypt." Unbelieving doubt requires that we spurn the past faithfulness of God. It asks us to ignore the command to "not forget all his benefits" (Ps. 103:2). In short, it requires us to disregard God's work and trust our own.

Do you think every person struggles with unbelieving doubt? Where do you see it in your own life?

What do you think the relationship is between unbelieving doubt and other sins or struggles?

Be

Personal Study 2

The fool says in his heart "there is no God."
PSALM 14:1 & PSALM 53:1

The fear of the Lord is the beginning of wisdom,
and the knowledge of the Holy One is understanding.
PROVERBS 9:10

Sometimes putting things in terms of "doubt" and "belief" makes them impersonal. It can sound intellectual, like a thought exercise or a problem to solve. But that's not how the Bible deals with unbelief. Scripture makes it clear that the defining thing about us is what we believe about God. So to discuss "unbelieving doubt" is no mere thought exercise or puzzle. It's a matter of life being rich and full or empty and hopeless.

How and why is what we believe about God
the most defining thing in our lives?

How does what you believe about God define your life?

In the previous study, we described unbelieving doubt as idolatry, the belief in self as the lord of life. How does this look in the midst of struggles?

Thinking God made a mistake.

Thinking God forgot something.

Thinking God was surprised by something

Thinking God isn't who He says He is in the Bible.

Thinking God hasn't or won't keep His promises.

Thinking that just because we don't understand something about God means it can't be understood.

Thinking God isn't good because He isn't doing what we want Him to do.

Thinking God owes us something.

Some of you doing this study might not believe there is a God. Most of you, however, do believe in God. And most of you who believe in God claim to follow Him. So let me pose this question:

What's the difference between believing we're the lord of our own lives and not believing in God at all?

If our doubts put us in a position where we no longer trust God, we question His motives, we wonder about His abilities, we're skeptical of His presence and power, and we mistrust His Word then what's the real, functional difference between these unbelieving doubts and not believing in God at all?

Psalm 14:1 and Psalm 53:1 begin the same way: "The fool says in his heart 'there is no God.'" In biblical terms, a fool is someone who rebels against God, who is wise in his own eyes, and thinks he knows best. This is the essence of unbelieving doubt. The rejection of God is foolishness, according to the Bible. But we need to understand that "foolishness" isn't the same as "stupidity" or "ignorance." Those are issues of knowledge and immaturity. Foolishness— as the Bible defines it—is sin leading to destruction. Unbelieving doubt is foolishness.

If foolishness is the rejection of God and leads to the way of destruction, what's biblical wisdom? What are its rewards?

Look at Proverbs 9:10, though. It offers a refrain that is woven throughout the pages of Proverbs and is reflected across all the books of the Bible.

The fear of the Lord is the beginning of wisdom.

To grasp the significance of this, we need to understand what "fear" and "wisdom" mean.

What does "fear of the Lord" mean?
Why is it a good thing for us?

To fear the Lord doesn't mean to cower or feel threatened. 1 John tells us that "perfect love casts out fear" and "God is love," so we know this can't be that kind of fear. Instead, imagine standing in the African Savannah and seeing a bull elephant striding toward you. You would be afraid, but you would be awed too. Now imagine standing on the brink of Angel Falls, the highest waterfall in the world at more than 3,000 feet. You would be weak in the knees at the height and the rush of water, but you would be overwhelmed by the beauty and majesty too. Now imagine meeting Queen Elizabeth of Great Britain, known for her diplomacy, gentility, and dignity. You would be nervous and overwhelmed by her position of royalty but also warmed and welcomed by her grace. Combine these, and we have the slightest sense of what it feels like to fear God.

What's the connection between fearing the Lord and doubt?

What makes fear of the Lord matter to us daily as we deal with hard questions and difficult or painful realities of life?

To fear the Lord is more than this too. To fear the Lord is to know and believe deep down in our souls what we laid out in the first session: God is infinite, all-powerful, and all good, and we aren't. So it is to live life according to the way and command of the God who knows best, plans best, works best, and has our best in mind. This is wisdom. Wisdom is to walk according to the way of the Lord, not the way of self. It's the way of hope and life.

Unbelieving doubt is foolish rebellion against the living God. It's not a mere exploration of ideas but rather a rejection of the truth that gives life. Believing in God is hard. Believing in God can be confusing. Sometimes it's scary—so is fearing the Lord. The difference is that the fear of the Lord brings into account the love of the Lord, which drives out other fears and is the way of wisdom, life, and hope.

Personal Study 3

While doubt isn't necessarily a sin, there's a great temptation for us to respond to it in such a way that it becomes sin. It's easy and natural to respond to difficult questions or circumstances with an attitude of pride and a mindset that we know best. Sometimes this is overt rebellion, and other times it's a quiet resignation that we can't believe God and His Word. Either way, when we struggle to find hope in God, we are like the fool who says in his heart, "there is no God" because a God we don't trust might as well not even exist. This is unbelieving doubt. Now is the time to do a frightening thing: examine your heart. Drag your doubts into the light to let the Word of God shine on them. See how He compares to things you fear and how He responds to the questions you struggle to answer.

When you read Hebrews 11:1, how do you make sense of the tension between the assurance it describes and the unknown it describes? How does that help you understand what it means to have faith?

When you read "a refusal to believe God is an affirmation that I know better," what does that look like in your life? In what areas of life do you act as if you know better than God?

How do you think doubts transition from an innocent starting place of "I don't know" to the place of unbelief that can't or won't trust God?

If you say you believe in God, but you can't or won't trust Him, what kind of God is He really?

What's the connection between faith, wisdom, and fear of the Lord? What do you need to pray for specifically to grow in these characteristics?

A great temptation for us is to respond to doubt in such a way that it becomes sin.

Week 3

Bring Your Doubt to Jesus

Start

Welcome to Session 3.

As you studied unbelieving doubt over the last week, what point or idea was the most helpful to you? Why?

In the last session, we looked particularly at the kinds of doubt that undermine and kill our faith, unbelieving doubt. Starting this week, we're going to begin to see how doubts can actually build our faith.

What do you do instinctively when you begin to struggle with doubt? What actions do you take?

For the next few sessions, we'll look at a story of a doubting man's interaction with Jesus from a few different angles to see what we can learn about how we should respond to doubts and how Jesus responds to us. We will begin to see how his response to doubt led him to help, hope, and faith in Jesus.

ASK SOMEONE TO PRAY THEN WATCH THE VIDEO TEACHING FOR SESSION 3.

Watch

Use this page to take notes during the video teaching.

Discuss

USE THE FOLLOWING QUESTIONS TO FACILITATE YOUR GROUP DISCUSSION.

Read Mark 9:14–17 together.

Where do you see yourself in this story of a father in need?

What could you learn about doubt and questions from this father's faith?

Why is it so hard to bring doubts and struggles to Jesus?

What does it look like for you to bring doubts to Jesus? What practical steps can you take to do that?

This session examined the story of a father facing an enormous struggle, dealing with massive doubts, and coming to Jesus for help. It's a story of faith that we should be able to find ourselves in. No, most of us don't have a demon-possessed child. But we do have problems we don't know how to resolve. The father recognized what he was dealing with reached beyond his capability, so He took his needs and doubts to Jesus. The question is: does our response to doubt resemble his?

What's the risk when we refuse to bring doubts to Jesus?

What experiences have you had in bringing hard things to Jesus? What has the result been?

CLOSE THE GROUP IN PRAYER. REMIND THE GROUP TO COMPLETE THE THREE PERSONAL STUDIES BEFORE THE NEXT MEETING.

Know

Personal Study 1

READ MARK 9:14-27.

And when they came to the disciples, they saw a great crowd around them, and scribes arguing with them. And immediately all the crowd, when they saw him, were greatly amazed and ran up to him and greeted him. And he asked them, "What are you arguing about with them?" And someone from the crowd answered him, "Teacher, I brought my son to you, for he has a spirit that makes him mute. And whenever it seizes him, it throws him down, and he foams and grinds his teeth and becomes rigid. So I asked your disciples to cast it out, and they were not able." And he answered them, "O faithless generation, how long am I to be with you? How long am I to bear with you? Bring him to me." And they brought the boy to him. And when the spirit saw him, immediately it convulsed the boy, and he fell on the ground and rolled about, foaming at the mouth. And Jesus asked his father, "How long has this been happening to him?" And he said, "From childhood. And it has often cast him into fire and into water, to destroy him. But if you can do anything, have compassion on us and help us." And Jesus said to him, "'If you can'! All things are possible for one who believes." Immediately the father of the child cried out and said, "I believe; help my unbelief!" And when Jesus saw that a crowd came running together, he rebuked the unclean spirit, saying to it, "You mute and deaf spirit, I command you, come out of him and never enter him again." And after crying out and convulsing him terribly, it came out, and the boy was like a corpse, so that most of them said, "He is dead." But Jesus took him by the hand and lifted him up, and he arose.

MARK 9:14-27

What stands out to you in this text, specifically about the father's actions and posture?

Think of the people you love most in the world: your spouse, children, friends, or family. Now imagine that one of them faced potential death every day. With no notice, he will experience a fit or seizure that could take his life. This has gone on for years, and you have tried everything in your power to help. You've taken him to doctors and specialists, you've taken him to psychiatrists and counselors, and you've met with pastors and prayed over him. And still, he suffers. And you suffer with him.

Put yourself in the shoes of the father in this story. How do you think he must've been feeling? What kinds of struggles was he bringing to Jesus?

The father in this story was helpless, exhausted, and afraid. All his efforts had come to nothing. As a father, he likely felt guilt and shame because he couldn't save his child from suffering. He was supposed to provide for and protect his children, and he could do nothing. He was powerless. Each day was an unknown, a frightening reality of uncertainty, and he had no idea when this cycle would come to an end or what possible end there would be besides disaster and tragedy.

So many of our doubts come from a similar circumstance. It may not be a child whom we can't help or heal, but the emotions and struggles are the same: fear, worry, fatigue, shame, guilt, helplessness. It's a context of all questions and no answers. Doubts thrive when we keep them to ourselves instead of taking them to Christ.

**What experiences or struggles have you had
that have stirred up doubts like this?**

The text isn't clear whether the father came to Jesus with his need as soon as he heard about Him or whether he was reluctant to approach Jesus. It doesn't say whether he had known about Jesus for months and hesitated out of fear and shame or whether he rushed to get help from Jesus the moment he heard about His miracles and ministry. It doesn't say whether he traveled a great distance or down the block. What it makes abundantly clear is that the man faced an overwhelming problem, struggled with doubts, and brought them to the feet of Jesus.

Why do you delay bringing your doubt to Jesus?

**How do your doubts fester and grow by not bringing
them to Jesus, so that He can deal with them?**

The father approached Jesus unabashedly. Not tentatively or privately. Not leaving his son behind lest he cause a scene. Not in secret and embarrassment like the religious leader, Nicodemus (John 3). The father came in a crowd, brought his son, and boldly asked for the help he needed. He even asked the disciples first, since Jesus wasn't there yet. He was in desperate need and willing to do what it took to get help. In short, the father's actions were the exact opposite of our most common instincts.

**What can we learn from the father about how
we can approach Jesus with doubts?**

The father was a model of obedience and faith. He modeled the kind of faith Hebrews 11:1 describes, "the assurance of things hoped for, the conviction of things not seen." He approached Jesus with boldness (assurance) and asked for help with clarity (conviction) in spite of the doubts he carried. He embodied faith. This story depicts how we should respond to doubt and the actions we should take.

**Do you feel free to come to Jesus with boldness and confidence
in your time of need like the father did? Why or why not?**

What doubts are you keeping from Jesus?

Some of you may just now be discovering the real Jesus. Some of you have known Jesus for a long time. Regardless, the actions of faith are the same. Come to Jesus with your doubts. He will respond with mercy and grace and the help you need. You'll find no answer to doubts and struggles elsewhere. Only Jesus can meet our desperate needs and answer our deepest questions

Be

Personal Study 2

Many of us acknowledge we should bring our doubts to Jesus, but mere acknowledgment isn't enough. We have to take action and actually bring our doubts to Jesus. In the first day of personal study, we put ourselves in the shoes of the father in the story—with all his fears, pains, and doubts. For many of us, this exercise was a thought experiment. However, for others of us, we don't need to imagine doubts; we wake up each morning with real doubts and questions.

While the father approached Jesus with clarity and boldness, our inclination is to do the exact opposite. When we carry the sort of burdens he bore—fatigue, fear, shame, guilt, helplessness, hopelessness—Jesus is often the last place we run. We fear rejection. We don't trust His promises. We forget all the accounts Scripture gives us of Jesus saving, helping, healing, restoring. Our sinful nature, the one that follows in the footsteps of Adam and Eve, gravitationally pulls away from Jesus.

What happens when you pull away from Jesus?

What leads you to pull away in the first place?

Sometimes we seek to hide our struggles. This may work with other people, but it will never work with God. We forget God is all-knowing and ever-present. It's impossible to hide anything from Him.

Sometimes we flee the presence of God. This might look like letting dust gather on our Bible, avoiding Christian community, and neglecting prayer. However, our doubts grow in proportion to our distance from God.

Sometimes we deny reality. We deny doubts and struggles, and suppress them in an attempt to fool ourselves and others. It's like a child who, when told to clean her room, shoves everything under the bed and announces, "I'm done." If she tries that enough times, eventually all the trash begins to spill out. The old juice boxes gather fruit flies, and the banana peel stinks to high heaven. When we deny the reality of our struggles, they turn into a putrid mess that eventually become obvious.

Sometimes we use a proxy for Jesus. We talk to friends, counselors, and pastors. These are all good things to do when doubting. It should not be struggled with alone. And when we rightly lean on people in our struggles, they point us back to the truth of Scripture and the hope of Jesus. But often those good things become substitutes for Jesus. If we're taking our struggles to good people but ignoring the Word of God, we're settling for less than the hope and help we truly need.

Why do the above tendencies seem like a better option to us than going to Jesus directly?

Counselors, friends, and pastors are all good gifts whom God gave us to help us. But how do you recognize when you're depending on them instead of Jesus?

All of the examples on the previous page are ultimately examples of depending on ourselves instead of God. Only after we've run through a multitude of these self-solutions do we stop and finally arrive at the conclusion that we need Jesus. He's our last resort.

He's also our best resort. Jesus is the only true hope for the struggling doubter. Yes, we can run, hide, or deny for a time, but nothing is resolved in our souls. In fact, usually the opposite happens, and things get worse. Yes, counselors and pastors and friends will help—in so much as they point back to the truth of Christ as found in the Bible. Anything shy of that, and they feed our dependence on idols and self.

What or whom are you currently depending on that isn't Jesus?

All our fears and hesitations, the same ones the father must have felt, aren't too great for Jesus. No shame is too deep. No struggle leaves a stain too dark. No web of questions is too tangled. No long-standing failure is too late. Jesus is the hope for it all. This is what the father realized in Mark 9, and what we must realize now. If you struggle to believe this, consider that the father brought a demon to Jesus. His doubts weren't just questions or fears. They were questions and fears about real, supernatural evil. And still, he came to Jesus. And Jesus helped him.

Jesus welcomes us with an open invitation. Jesus will help our doubts in the ways we need most.

End today thanking Jesus for welcoming your questions and doubts. Use this time to express any lingering doubts to Him.

Jesus is the only true hope for the struggling doubter.

Do

Personal Study 3

This session potentially poked a nerve, and a sensitive one at that. It dug into the shame and fear of doubt, and that's not something anyone enjoys. But it's something each of us needs. Left to our own devices, we will, well, depend on our own devices. That's where we go wrong in handling doubt. Instead, we need the nudge (or shove) to respond as the father did in Mark 9. We need the impetus to depend and the reminder that it's so much more hopeful to do so. And we need the assurance that the discomfort is worth it. That's part of the reason such stories are in the Bible, as a reminder that difficulties are real, faith is necessary, and there's real promise in that faith. Doing the hard, faithful thing is right, even when it's scary or exhausting.

Rest in that promise as you reflect on and answer these questions:

Why do we feel so much guilt and shame about doubt, especially since it's common to every person? What does this indicate about how we see Jesus and what we believe about him?

When you think about bringing doubts to Jesus, what do you truly believe will happen?

What struggles and doubts do you have that seem too great, too longstanding, too complicated for Jesus? What would it take for you to bring these to Him?

What practical steps can you take to bring doubts to Jesus? What habits can you work on developing or people can you partner with so this becomes a first response to doubt instead of a last resort?

Any solution to a struggle that does not depend on God is dependence on self.

Week 4
Admit Your Struggle

Start

Welcome to Session 4.

**As you worked through the personal studies
last week, what's one doubt you found
that you needed to bring to Jesus?**

In the last session, we examined the actions of the father in this story. We saw how he approached Jesus and the context in which he did so. His actions spoke loudly of faith and dependence. It was a clear example to us of how to respond in times of doubt and struggle. It's the father's words, though, that stand out the most in this passage, one prayer in particular.

**Why is it so hard for us to admit
what we're struggling with?**

In this session, we'll examine this prayer. We will see it as an invitation to doubters, an encouragement to believers, and a standard up to which we can live.

**ASK SOMEONE TO PRAY THEN WATCH
THE VIDEO TEACHING FOR SESSION 4.**

Watch

Use this page to take notes during the video teaching.

USE THE FOLLOWING QUESTIONS TO FACILITATE YOUR GROUP DISCUSSION.

Read Mark 9:14–27.

The father in this story could be described as a humble seeker. Jesus expects this same attitude from us. He wants us to come to Him with humility. But He wants us to come with clarity too. Humility isn't hesitance; it's an attitude of belief that acknowledges His greatness, our need, His perfection, and our sinfulness. When we come to Jesus as the father did, we can make requests and express our needs with boldness—not demanding but open and clear.

Read Luke 18:9–14. What does this show us about how we should approach God and speak to Him?

What's the difference between pride and boldness when we approach Jesus with our needs?

What leads us to approach Jesus with pride as opposed to boldness?

In what false or inappropriate ways do you come to Jesus?

Why is the prayer, "I believe; help my unbelief" actually a statement of faith?

Where do you need to utilize this prayer in your own life?

CLOSE THE GROUP IN PRAYER. REMIND THE GROUP TO COMPLETE THE THREE PERSONAL STUDIES BEFORE THE NEXT MEETING.

Know

Personal Study 1

READ MARK 9:14-27.

And when they came to the disciples, they saw a great crowd around them, and scribes arguing with them. And immediately all the crowd, when they saw him, were greatly amazed and ran up to him and greeted him. And he asked them, "What are you arguing about with them?" And someone from the crowd answered him, "Teacher, I brought my son to you, for he has a spirit that makes him mute. And whenever it seizes him, it throws him down, and he foams and grinds his teeth and becomes rigid. So I asked your disciples to cast it out, and they were not able." And he answered them, "O faithless generation, how long am I to be with you? How long am I to bear with you? Bring him to me." And they brought the boy to him. And when the spirit saw him, immediately it convulsed the boy, and he fell on the ground and rolled about, foaming at the mouth. And Jesus asked his father, "How long has this been happening to him?" And he said, "From childhood. And it has often cast him into fire and into water, to destroy him. But if you can do anything, have compassion on us and help us." And Jesus said to him, "'If you can'! All things are possible for one who believes." Immediately the father of the child cried out and said, "I believe; help my unbelief!" And when Jesus saw that a crowd came running together, he rebuked the unclean spirit, saying to it, "You mute and deaf spirit, I command you, come out of him and never enter him again." And after crying out and convulsing him terribly, it came out, and the boy was like a corpse, so that most of them said, "He is dead." But Jesus took him by the hand and lifted him up, and he arose.

MARK 9:14-27

Notice how the father spoke to Jesus in this passage. First, the father was forthright and transparent. There was no hemming and hawing and trying to make his situation sound better than it is. He didn't hold back or beat around the bush. He made his need known.

What obstacles do you face in being honest about your needs, either to other people or in prayer to God?

Second, he wasn't brash or demanding, but humble. Often boldness and clarity are expressed in a demanding way like we are owed something. The father didn't speak that way. His honesty was actually detrimental to his own image. He wasn't making demands or seeking to be seen as strong. He was bold in his need for help, that is, for childlike faith, and it honored Jesus.

How can we be clear and forthright in our expressions of need without being selfish, prideful, or demanding?

Third, he was self-aware. The father knew his weakness and inability to save his son. He recognized his need for Jesus. If he had harbored any sense of strength, power, or ability to resolve the situation, he couldn't have asked what he did. But because he looked at himself and saw utter inability, he was able to pray the prayer that stands out so much in these verses.

How do we cultivate an understanding of our limitations so that we turn to Jesus readily? What does it mean for our relationship with Jesus?

Verse 24 is where we find this prayer: "I believe; help my unbelief." For every other notable thing we've seen about this story—the father's actions, posture, and tone—this simple sentence is the cornerstone for understanding doubt. He could have said, "please help me," "I believe you can help me," or "I'm struggling and need help." Those would have been true words, genuine prayers. But they wouldn't have captured the full spectrum of what it means to believe when we aren't sure.

**How does this short prayer encapsulate our
relationship with the infinite, perfect God?**

In five words, the father prays a prayer on which faith hinges. All faith, no matter how great or small. Think back on session one, where we saw that doubt stems from the reality of an infinitely perfect God and finite, sinful people. At its beginning, doubt is, "I don't know." This prayer lives in that reality because it expressef belief in the powerful God and admitted struggle with what he didn't know how to believe.

This prayer resounds with conviction and assurance: "I believe." And it's rife with things hoped for and not yet seen: "Help my unbelief." It's a lived-out, embodied expression of what the Bible defines as true faith. And that means it's a prayer for each of us.

**Compare Hebrews 11:1 with Mark 9:24. How do both
point to the coexistence of doubt and faith?**

When you read the word "confession," you likely think of sin or something shameful because it's most commonly used to be just that—admitting guilt. But confession has a second meaning: to express clearly what you believe. In this verse, we see a double confession. The second half is what we usually think of, an admission of something undesirable—help my unbelief. It's a confession both of need and unbelief. The first half of the verse, however, is a confession of the other sort as it declares belief. It's a confession as a profession of faith.

This tension is so rich and vital for us to understand as we seek to grow in faith. Faith isn't the absence of doubt but the right response to it. This prayer models that by first confessing belief in Jesus and second confessing doubt, struggle, and need. "I believe; help my unbelief" is a prayer of faith, for and from faith. It's a prayer for those mired in doubt and for those in a place of peace. It's a prayer for you.

In the next study, we'll explore how to pray this prayer and what it means in the life of a believer.

When you reflect on the prayer, "I believe; help my unbelief," which confession do you resonate with more—"I believe" or "help my unbelief"?

Which do you struggle with more? Why?

Be

Personal study 2

How far can a five-word prayer take you? It seems like it might use up its meaning pretty quickly. Or maybe it will turn into a mantra and be rotely repeated. We can get bored with whole books of the Bible, so what chance does a prayer like, "I believe; help my unbelief," stand in staying pertinent, fresh, and applicable?

What's the difference between meditating on the words of Scripture and repeating them like a mantra—speaking them over and over again in the hope they become true?

This isn't a prayer like any other, though. It's a paradigm as much as it's a request. It's a framework for faith and belief in the midst of anything. And for that reason, "I believe; help my unbelief" is always pertinent, fresh, and true.

How does this prayer help you understand the very nature of faith?

We see in this story an instance of when this prayer can be prayed: at wit's end, when all else has been tried and proved wanting, and there are no more answers except Jesus. It's a prayer for desperate times when your faith is on the brink of failing. It's a prayer for exhausting times when you are not sure you can hold on to belief much longer. It's a prayer for those times of fog when you can't see the truth of God's Word or sense His presence. It's a prayer for times of temptation when sin seems so appealing, and you aren't sure it's worth resisting.

And it's a prayer for when things are good, and you're grateful because in those moments you should celebrate "I believe," and acknowledge there's still unbelief in your heart. Because good times are when we're most prone not to rely on God. Remember, the prayer is a double confession, one part proclamation of what we believe and the other an admission of where we have need.

How does this prayer help you when your faith is weak?

How does this prayer help you when your faith is strong?

The first two words, "I believe," are a statement to God that you do trust Him, His Word, and His character. It's an affirmation you believe He keeps His promises and that He is who He says He is. To pray this, you don't have to believe all of this perfectly (in fact, you never will this side of heaven). You just need to believe it as well as you can in the moment. To pray this prayer at all is an act of belief because it shows you believe there's a God who hears you and might act on your behalf. That's a seed of faith.

How is it encouraging that we won't believe perfectly in this life?

The last three words, "help my unbelief," are a plea for help. None of us ever believes as we ought. And often, we barely believe at all. We struggle to see the truth of God's Word or to trust that He will do what He says He will do. We struggle to understand what the Bible says, and we are tempted to believe lies and walk headlong into sin or give up on Christianity all together. So we need the prayer, "help my unbelief." We need it today, tomorrow, the next day, and the day after that. We need it constantly because we regularly struggle with unbelief.

What does your struggle with unbelief look like? In what areas of your life do you particularly need to apply this prayer?

This prayer is a paradigm for faith because it relieves the pressure of having all the answers. Often we feel like we must know what to think and what to do in every situation. We think we must be able to explain every mysterious thing about God or complex passage from Scripture. Faith says that not only do we not have to do these things, we are not able to. We can't have all the answers because we are not God. So we have faith. And we have this prayer.

How might praying this prayer ease a burden for you?

When we pray, "I believe; help my unbelief," we are doing the most faithful thing a person can do. We are expressing the assurance and confidence we have in God—sometimes much, sometimes little—and we are confessing that we are limited, sinful, and need Jesus' help. What else is there for a Christian? We believe, and we need Jesus. Constantly, in all situations and every struggle. And so God gave us this prayer and showed us how it can be spoken to Jesus whenever and wherever we need.

The five-word prayer, "I believe; help my unbelief," is in many ways the hinge on which faith turns.

Do

Personal Study 3

This session revolves almost entirely around five words. But it also draws on the beliefs and attitudes the father exhibits as he speaks to Jesus. "I believe; help my unbelief," is more than just a sentence; it's reflective of the entire journey of growing in faith as a Christian. It's a constant prayer for us, no matter what stage in life we're in or the health of our faith.

If we are a follower of Jesus, we do believe, even if it's feeble sometimes. If we can pray, we do believe God hears our prayer. We may struggle to trust. We may not be clear on what we believe or how to express it. We may not even always be sure we're Christians, but if we can sincerely pray this prayer, then it means there's belief in us, and Jesus won't reject or push us away.

As human beings, we need help with our unbelief. We can't overcome it ourselves. We need the Holy Spirit to help us see and believe the real, magnificent Jesus. God loves when we pray this prayer because it 's an invitation for His Spirit to work in us.

**In what areas of life do you need to grow
both humility and boldness?**

What aspects of God and His Word do you need
to reflect on to bolster your belief? What do you
need to cling to when you pray, "I believe"?

In what particular areas of life or thought do
you need to pray "help my unbelief?"

How has this study helped you live comfortably
in the tension between faith and doubt?

*We all need help
with our unbelief.
We cannot
overcome it
ourselves.*

Week 5

Jesus' Response to Doubt

Start

Welcome to Session 5.

What's your main takeaway from our last two sessions studying the father from Mark 9?

In the last two sessions, we emphasized a secondary character and didn't give much attention to the hero of the story. The father in Mark 9 isn't the main character or the most important person. But he's the character we most relate to, the one who is in a position with which we can understand.

Jesus is the main character in this story. He's the object of faith. How Jesus responds to doubters is of utmost importance. It doesn't matter how we respond to doubt, how we wrestle with it, how we seek to understand it if we can't trust that Jesus will be gracious to us. In this session we'll study (and revel in) how Jesus responds to doubters.

How has this study helped you become more comfortable with taking your doubts to Jesus?

ASK SOMEONE TO PRAY THEN WATCH THE VIDEO TEACHING FOR SESSION 5.

Watch

Use this page to take notes during the video teaching.

USE THE FOLLOWING QUESTIONS TO FACILITATE YOUR GROUP DISCUSSION.

Read Mark 9:14–27 together.

Jesus loves doubters. He doesn't turn us away or reject us. He's gracious, kind, and patient. He doesn't get tired of our questions or struggles. If we come to Him in humility, He always welcomes us and corrects us. He understands us in our doubt but isn't willing to let us languish there. He comes to us and meets our needs.

How did Jesus respond to the father's prayer and plea for help? What should that communicate to us about how He handles our doubts?

Scripture teaches that Jesus welcomes us, even in our doubts. What do you believe about Jesus that makes you think He might not welcome you in your doubts?

What do you believe about yourself that makes you think Jesus might not welcome you in your doubts?

How has Jesus corrected your doubts in the past?

What means or methods does Jesus use to correct you?

Are you OK with Jesus giving you what you need in order to believe even if it's not what you want?

CLOSE THE GROUP IN PRAYER. REMIND THE GROUP TO COMPLETE THE THREE PERSONAL STUDIES BEFORE THE NEXT MEETING.

Help My Unbelief

Jesus loves doubters in the truest sense. He doesn't just welcome us; He corrects us.

Know

Personal study 1

READ MARK 9:14-27.

And when they came to the disciples, they saw a great crowd around them, and scribes arguing with them. And immediately all the crowd, when they saw him, were greatly amazed and ran up to him and greeted him. And he asked them, "What are you arguing about with them?" And someone from the crowd answered him, "Teacher, I brought my son to you, for he has a spirit that makes him mute. And whenever it seizes him, it throws him down, and he foams and grinds his teeth and becomes rigid. So I asked your disciples to cast it out, and they were not able." And he answered them, "O faithless generation, how long am I to be with you? How long am I to bear with you? Bring him to me." And they brought the boy to him. And when the spirit saw him, immediately it convulsed the boy, and he fell on the ground and rolled about, foaming at the mouth. And Jesus asked his father, "How long has this been happening to him?" And he said, "From childhood. And it has often cast him into fire and into water, to destroy him. But if you can do anything, have compassion on us and help us." And Jesus said to him, "'If you can'! All things are possible for one who believes." Immediately the father of the child cried out and said, "I believe; help my unbelief!" And when Jesus saw that a crowd came running together, he rebuked the unclean spirit, saying to it, "You mute and deaf spirit, I command you, come out of him and never enter him again." And after crying out and convulsing him terribly, it came out, and the boy was like a corpse, so that most of them said, "He is dead." But Jesus took him by the hand and lifted him up, and he arose.
MARK 9:14-27

How does Jesus respond to this struggling father?

When we hear Jesus, we hear the voice of God. When He speaks, we need to lean in and pay attention. Notice the progression in Christ's words in this text. First, He engaged in a way that makes the father feel welcome and willing to open up. Jesus began with a question and gave the father the opportunity to speak in faith. Jesus stepped into a chaotic crowd and created a context in which He could listen and act.

What do we learn about the compassionate heart of God toward doubters through Jesus' response?

Next, Jesus corrected—"O faithless generation" (Mark 9:19). This wasn't an insult but a plea for belief. Jesus looked over the crowd, and specifically at His disciples and called them to faith. He pointed out their lack, so they would be able to see that He could fill it.

What made Jesus feel the need to so clearly, vocally correct the people?

We know Jesus wasn't just casting judgment and getting fed up because the next words out of His mouth were an invitation—"Bring him to me." At first glance, this could be read as exasperation. But that doesn't mesh with the tone and what follows. By telling the father to bring the boy, Jesus showed that He was more than willing to embrace the problem that was causing so much pain. Jesus embraced the overwhelming circumstance.

What doubts or struggles do you need to bring to Jesus?

After hearing from the father the full nature of the problem, Jesus provided assurance—"'If you can'! All things are possible for one who believes" (Mark 9:23). The father is hesitant, wondering, worrying, doubting, and Jesus boldly declared His power to act on behalf of all who trust in Him.

We are often like the father, bringing things to Jesus hesitantly, and wondering if He can help. How does His declaration encourage you in your struggles?

The final words of Jesus' recorded here are a command—"he rebuked the unclean spirit, saying to it, 'You mute and deaf spirit, I command you, come out of him and never enter him again" (Mark 9:25). Jesus declared His authority over evil, darkness, doubt, and fear, and He banished it. He spoke darkness away and shone His light in. Jesus did precisely what was needed for the doubting man. He did it without placing any conditions or demands on the father.

What evils or struggles in your life do you have a hard time believing Jesus has authority and power over?

Do you believe Jesus will meet your needs with no caveats or conditions? Why or why not?

There is so much to observe from this text, but I want to focus on one particular aspect. While Jesus welcomes anyone with honest, humble doubts and while He doesn't condemn or crush the struggler, He also doesn't let doubters stay where they are. Jesus is neither apathetic about our faith nor content to let us doubt.

It's notable what we don't see in this text—what Jesus didn't say. When the father comes to Jesus, he does not hear, "Oh, that's OK; you'll make it." Jesus didn't tell him he was doing fine or to "stay strong." Jesus neither lets the father wallow, nor did He crush him. Instead, Jesus gently corrected. Jesus listened, then He lovingly guided the father toward the truth. This is how Jesus responds to doubters.

Jesus perfectly models speaking the truth in love. How does your response to those who are doubting compare to Jesus'?

What does it look like for us to do that for those who are struggling and doubting?

For a moment, consider Thomas in John 20. Thomas vocalized his doubt; he couldn't believe in the resurrection unless He saw the wounds in Jesus' hands and side (John 20:25). When Jesus next appeared, He did two things: first, He showed Thomas the wounds while calling Him to faith, then He corrected Thomas. "Have you believed because you have seen me? Blessed are those who have not seen and yet have believed" (John 20:29). Jesus wouldn't let Thomas stay in unbelief. He did what Thomas needed and called him to better and greater faith.

Consider Peter. On the night that Jesus was betrayed, Peter stood outside His trial and denied knowing Jesus three times, each time with greater vehemence and concluding with a profane tirade (John 20:25–27). After

Jesus rose from the dead, how did He respond to Peter? John 21 tells us how He pulled Peter aside and asked three times, "do you love me?" Each time Peter responds that he did, that Jesus knew he did, and each time Jesus commissioned Peter to care for the flock of believers (John 21:15–19). In this conversation, we see Jesus drawing a confession of faith from Peter; it was a gentle reproof and clear course correction. It defined Peter by love and belief, not by denial of Jesus. And in calling Peter to "feed my sheep," Jesus declared that he's forgiven and restored.

Reflect on the stories of Thomas and Peter and how Jesus responded to their doubts. Which story most resonates with you? What's particularly encouraging?

What do you see of Jesus in these stories that you need in the midst of your doubts?

When we bring our doubts to Jesus, He responds the same way for us. He doesn't condemn or crush. Neither does He pander or allow us to stay in our doubts. He meets our needs and adjusts our trajectory. Doubt isn't a destination; it's a struggle and a mark of our need for wholeness in Christ. Jesus moves us towards wholeness with gentle corrections, reminders of love, and a clear calling to believe and obey. When we bring our doubts to Jesus, He welcomes us, speaks truth into our confusion, and He speaks correction that will change who we are and how we believe.

How does it help you to know that Jesus both welcomes you in your struggles and won't let you remain in them if you bring them to Him?

Be

Personal Study 2

One of the most consistent mistakes we make when we're doubting is to assume we know how God should respond. We think we know what we need, or what would help us most. When we have this attitude, we approach God as though He were a waiter ready to take our order and not the Creator and Sustainer of all things. In reality, we should cast ourselves on His mercy.

**Why do we so easily assume that we know
the best way to resolve our struggles?**

How does this assumption actually go against faith?

In Mark 9, the father came to Jesus with a specific request but also with faith. He didn't act as if he knew what was best but rather postured himself as dependent. This is the stance of faith, and it's vital for us to recognize it because otherwise we miss the point of this story.

**How does dependence better position us to
receive God's answers to our prayers?**

Jesus will always meet our needs and respond to a humble request for help. But Jesus won't always give us exactly what we ask for or what we think is best. In the case of this story, He did because to cast out the demon was to overcome evil and show He was worthy of faith. Often though, showing He is worthy of our faith does not look like fulfilling our specific desires. Jesus knows a better way to meet our needs even if it doesn't appear better to us.

> **It's easy to give mental assent to "Jesus knows better," but what does it look like to trust in that truth when we're in the midst of doubts?**

Paul says:

> *So to keep me from becoming conceited because of the surpassing greatness of the revelations, a thorn was given me in the flesh, a messenger of Satan to harass me, to keep me from becoming conceited. Three times I pleaded with the Lord about this, that it should leave me. But he said to me, "My grace is sufficient for you, for my power is made perfect in weakness." Therefore I will boast all the more gladly of my weaknesses, so that the power of Christ may rest upon me. For the sake of Christ, then, I am content with weaknesses, insults, hardships, persecutions, and calamities. For when I am weak, then I am strong.*
> **2 CORINTHIANS 12:7–10**

Paul described a hardship, given by God, that he specifically asked God to remove. Paul was in pain and a place of difficulty, so naturally, he assumed the best thing for him would be to have the thorn removed. God knew better. The pain had a purpose, and His power would be perfected in Paul by carrying him through it rather than removing it. God perfecting His power means, in part, letting it be seen in strengthened faith and increased perseverance. Paul was drawn closer to Jesus, was more dependent on Him, and grew in humility and faith through God answering Paul's prayer differently than he asked.

We usually want God to show His power by fixing our problems or answering our questions. How is God's power shown more clearly in our weakness?

When has your own weakness provided an avenue for God to work and display His glory?

The same is true for us. The question, then, is whether we are willing to accept this.

In the first session, we saw that God is infinite and perfect. His wisdom is too wonderful for us; it's beyond our comprehension. At a conceptual level, that sounds wonderful and worthy of our trust. But amid doubts and trials, it's a reality that's sometimes much harder to find peace in. It often means the answers or relief we want isn't forthcoming because God knows a better way (the best way) we can't see.

Faith clings to the truth that God is doing what we need, what's best, what will bring us through, regardless if we can see how He's doing so. Faith trusts that His power is perfected in our weakness and that it's for our good.

What's the difference between "blind faith" and having assurance and confidence when we can't see what God is doing?

Jesus always meets the needs of those who trust Him whether it's in an obvious, victorious way as He did in Mark 9 or in an opaque, mysterious way as Paul described in 2 Corinthians 12. Will we trust? Will we cling to every truth we know about Jesus as forgiver, redeemer, savior, and sender of the Holy Spirit, who is our Helper? Will we be people of faith even when we don't see?

His power is perfected in our weakness. His answer to "Help my unbelief" is always a resounding "YES." And His way of doing this is always perfect and for our best.

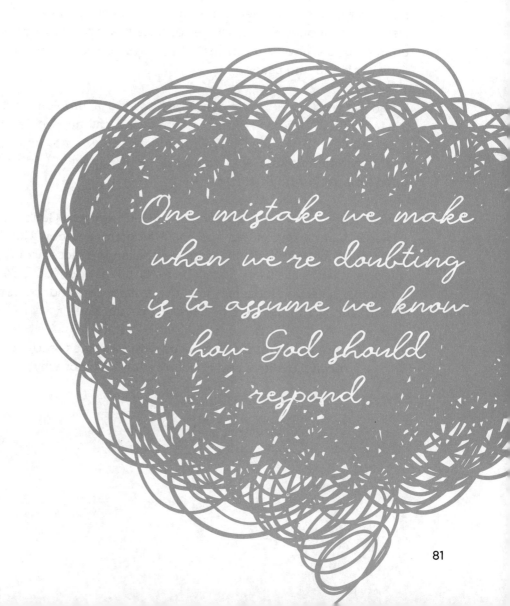

One mistake we make when we're doubting is to assume we know how God should respond.

Do

Personal Study 3

Jesus' response to doubts is both more and less than we ask. It's more because He's always doing infinitely more than we ask or imagine (Eph. 3:20). It's less because it often isn't what we specifically ask for. But His response to our struggles is always right, just, and always best. Our struggle is often to accept this and find peace in it.

When we read Mark 9, we see Jesus solving a problem and meeting a need. But we also see Him correcting and calling people to faith. In 2 Corinthians 12, we see God giving a perfect answer to doubts, but of a distinctly different kind. In both cases, God is perfectly right and is doing good for people who trust Him.

A vital facet of faith is the acceptance of God's will and God's Word. These passages paint a mysterious and beautiful picture of how God loves and cares for doubters and one that can be a challenge to accept and rest in. But that's what faith calls us to. Reflect on that truth as you work through these questions. Reflect on the mercy and love Jesus shows and the ways He may be correcting your heart and beliefs to grow your faith.

Are you approaching Jesus with struggles ready to receive His love and His correction? Why or why not?

What gentle correction might Jesus be giving you right now?

What passage or story from Scripture offers
you the most encouragement that Jesus won't
reject you because of your doubts?

How does Jesus' response to the father in Mark 9
(and others in Scripture) encourage you in your faith?

What struggles are you keeping from God right now?

What does this indicate about your view of Jesus?

Week 6

Doubts and Deeper Faith

Start

Welcome to Session 6.

**How did last week increase your confidence
in Jesus' ability to meet you in your doubt?**

In this final session, we have one lingering question. It was posed early in the study, it has been answered indirectly throughout, but we would be remiss if we allowed you to complete this study without a clear answer. The question is this: how do doubts bring us into deeper faith?

Earlier, we saw the other side of this, how doubts erode faith. Now we'll examine how they can build faith. We'll examine our hearts, our attitudes, and finally the very object of our faith—Jesus Christ. What better ending could there be to a study on faith and doubt than that?

**Share a time when overcoming
doubt helped build your faith.**

**ASK SOMEONE TO PRAY THEN WATCH
THE VIDEO TEACHING FOR SESSION 6.**

Watch

Use this page to take notes during the video teaching.

USE THE FOLLOWING QUESTIONS TO FACILITATE YOUR GROUP DISCUSSION.

As this study draws to a close, you have developed a clearer understanding about how God and doubt relate to one another. Hopefully you see doubt in a more serious way but also in a more hopeful one, an understanding of it that allows you a way forward and frees you from needless guilt. Hopefully you see Jesus more clearly, both as a glorious God, and a warm Savior—for He is both. Jesus is more powerful than our doubts. He is wiser than our questions. And He loves us more fiercely than we doubt Him.

How has this study helped you understand and respond to doubts and struggles in your life?

What do you need to change about how you bring questions to God?

When you take questions to God, do you feel guilty and ashamed or free and loved? What might this indicate about your perspective, heart, and attitude toward God?

Discuss the difference between "unbelieving doubt" and "believing doubt."

Which do you err towards more often? How has this study helped?

As we move on from this study, what are some ways we can help one another process our doubts and questions in a way that builds faith?

CLOSE THE GROUP IN PRAYER. REMIND THE GROUP TO COMPLETE THE THREE PERSONAL STUDIES.

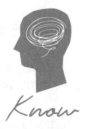

Know

Personal Study 1

How do doubts bring us into deeper faith? The very question seems contradictory, but it's not. Just as there are doubts that erode faith there are doubts that point us toward faith. It's not the substance of the doubt that makes the difference though. It's the response to the doubts in our souls, attitudes, prayers, and actions. The exact same question or doubt could lead a person either closer to Christ or further from Him. The question isn't the issue; the response is.

**What kind of response (heart, attitude, actions)
do you think turns doubters toward Jesus?**

**How does it help clarify things for you to think of
doubt as something that begins as neutral, neither
good nor bad, then having a specific trajectory?**

Unbelieving doubt thinks it knows better than God—like Adam and Eve in the garden in Genesis 3. Ultimately the doubter wants to be his or her own god, so if they encounter something He says or does they dislike or don't understand their doubt is that of a skeptic and a challenger. It's arrogant doubt marked by a reluctance to listen and a certainty of correctness. Unbelieving doubt refuses to believe or submit to God's Word.

Can a Christian struggle with unbelieving doubt? Why or why not?

Believing doubt, on the other hand, is marked primarily by humility. It begins with "I don't know" and its trajectory is toward the infinite God who has all wisdom. When it asks questions it seeks to listen and learn rather than challenge. It wants to know more of God rather than assuming it knows all it needs to. And believing doubt sees God's Word as the highest, final authority even if it struggles to understand.

What is the difference between belief and believing doubt?

In Mark 9 we encountered the seminal prayer, "I believe; help my unbelief." This is the heart and expression of believing doubt. Believing doubt holds fast to what it knows to be true about God and His Word even as it struggles to understand or accept other things about Him. It recognizes its own limitations and inability to fully understand God, but rather than resenting God for that, it trusts in Him. It knows its own propensity to rebel and move toward unbelieving doubt, so it prays "help my unbelief."

That can't be the prayer of unbelieving doubt because unbelieving doubt doesn't believe nor does it want to. It thinks it has the necessary answers, or at least that God lacks them. Either way there's no asking for help with unbelief, only demanding clarity or help or answers.

Who in Scripture notably exemplified believing doubt? How do they encourage you?

Throughout Scripture we see numerous examples of this kind of doubt (and plenty of the unbelieving variety as well). So many of the Psalms have a structure that begins with doubt—"How long O Lord?" (Ps. 13) "Why have you forsaken me?,"(Ps. 23) "Be not far from me" (Ps. 71)—and ends with an expression of trust or praise. In a single prayer we see doubt and belief, uncertainty and faith.

Last session we looked at Paul's words in 2 Corinthians 12 where he asked for a thorn to be removed, but the Lord did not remove it. Instead He assured Paul that "My power is perfected in weakness." Paul's response is trust, worship, and boasting in his weaknesses because that's where God is on display. Paul asked, Paul was denied, Paul continued to suffer, God gave assurance, Paul held on to hope and joy. That's believing doubt.

There are many other instances of people who obeyed God with trepidation but not hesitation, people like Abraham and Isaiah. Scripture doesn't describe their state of mind when they were called in detail, but the narrative makes clear they were unsure and even anxious but obeyed in faith any how. That's believing doubt because it doesn't see the whole picture, isn't sure of the future, but follows God's call regardless.

Throughout his life and leadership Moses approached God with questions and complaints. Other times he acted impulsively and ignored God's instructions. He exemplified doubt on both sides, often believing but sometimes unbelieving. And he was the man God used to lead his people from slavery to freedom and establish them as a nation!

Faith grows in certainty over time because it gains understanding about its object.

How does it encourage you to realize that many of the people God used most profoundly in Scripture were doubters?

How does it challenge you to see how they responded when they doubted?

Time and again Scripture gives us these examples, and they should encourage us. Doubt is common to all people, even heroes of the faith and leaders of God's people. What they have in common is the consistency with which they respond to doubts with humility, by turning to God instead of away, and by trusting in Him even when they do not understand. No doubt, these same biblical characters fell into unbelieving doubt sometimes as well. The Psalmists certainly did, so did Abraham, Moses, and even Paul (read Romans 7). But their trajectory, consistently, was toward God and His Word.

Believing doubt isn't certainty, but it is faith. And faith grows in certainty over time because it gains understanding about its object. Sometimes believing doubt is a reaching, grasping thing looking for those truths about which it can declare "I believe." But as we grow in it, believing doubt becomes more constantly confident in those truths it believes so that when uncertainty, trouble, and doubts come it can boldly state "I believe" and know that the prayer "help my unbelief" is already being answered.

Do you feel more like your believing doubt is reaching and grasping or confident and on a firm footing? Why?

Be

Personal Study 2

It's one thing to describe believing doubt and lay out its promises and merit, but for those of you struggling with doubts this might sound like some sort of candyland fairytale-esque fantasy. Sure it would be lovely to respond to doubt so well and cling so readily to biblical truths, but it's never that easy.

**When you read or hear faith described, does it seem
unattainable or difficult? Why or why not?**

Clinging to truth is difficult. Genuine faith is hard won; it isn't always easy and carefree. The very reason we need faith is life isn't carefree, doubts are heavy, and struggles hurt. So how do we adjust the trajectory of our doubts toward believing doubt and away from self-focus and self-belief?

**Is your inclination to try to change your own mind
and heart to adjust toward God? What are the effects
of this, decreased doubt or increased doubt?**

The answer is not found in a seven step process or a quick formula. Faith is never formulaic. The answer is to grow in biblical humility, the kind that

We move toward
faith when we stare
God in the face
by looking deeply
into His Word.

recognizes who God really is and who we really are. Humility and the faith it produces isn't something we can create in ourselves. For that, we need the Holy Spirit, the third person of the Godhead who Jesus calls our Teacher and Helper. The Spirit speaks to us and teaches us primarily through God's Word.

> **When someone reminds you to turn to Scripture to strengthen your faith, do you find that encouraging or tiresome? Why do you think this is?**

> **What does the Bible give us that nothing else can?**

The Bible is so complex and rich that it can sometimes be difficult to know where to look or what to look for when we're struggling. Let me offer three categories to remember when engaging the Bible. The Holy Spirit doesn't need categories to speak truth into us and transform our hearts, but sometimes they help us understand God in a way that offers clarity.

First, Scripture tells us of God's actions. We see story after story of what God has done on our behalf. He created the world, formed a people for Himself, made covenants and kept them, freed His people, won battles, fed, clothed, protected, sent prophets and messengers to guide and warn, disciplined His people toward repentance, and sent His Son to save us from our sins. He doesn't act on a whim, and He never acts inconsistently with His character. He's the same yesterday, today, and forever (Heb. 13:8).

> **What stories of God acting on behalf of His people are most encouraging to you in times of struggle?**

Secondly, we look to Scripture to find God's character. His character is why we can trust Him; it's His nature and reflects His very identity as God. He's holy, totally other from everything else in perfection, righteousness, flawless morality, and infinite glory. God's character is what we rest in and where His actions flow from.

What stops us from resting in the perfection and constancy of God's character?

From God's character also flow His promises, and that's the third category we can look for in Scripture. Over and over again, God makes definitive statements to His people of what He'll do for them and how He'll act toward them. He promises that every Word of His is true (Prov. 30:5). He promised to send a Savior (Isa. 9:6). He promises to never leave or forsake us (Heb. 13:5). God's promises are His declaration, out loud, of His character and His ongoing action on our behalf. Every promise is trustworthy, and your doubts or struggles cannot overcome that.

What particular promises in Scripture do you cling to when you're struggling? What promises do you struggle to believe?

So how do we move toward faith, toward believing doubt? We stare God in the face by looking deeply into His Word. It's where we find the assurance in "the assurance of things hoped for" as well as knowing what to hope for in the first place. It's where we find the "conviction of things not seen" and begin to understand that "unseen" means God is working in infinite goodness for our benefit and His glory. It's where we're given prayers like "I believe; help my unbelief" that we can take with us into every part of life. As we look into Scripture, the Holy Spirit will change our hearts and minds and give us sight. God calls us to faith, and He will give us faith if we look to Him.

Do

Personal Study 3

This session is the "go and sin no more" of this study. It's the commissioning to a better, stronger, more honest, humble faith. You'll always struggle with doubts. Sometimes they'll be subtle, and other times they'll hit you like a fully loaded U-Haul truck then back over you again. How will you respond? What will you cling to? What will you believe in the midst of doubts as your anchor and your lifeline?

Always remember to take your doubts to Jesus; He welcomes you. State them with humble boldness, declaring your need for His help; you have no other hope but Jesus. Reflect on the greatness and wonder and majesty of God; it will put things in proper perspective when you're tempted to self-aggrandizement. Mull over the promises of God and dedicate yourself to remembering His works, both in Scripture and in your life; this is the ballast when the storm of doubt threatens to capsize you.

Your doubts don't have to separate you from Jesus. They don't need to burden you with guilt and shame or have a corrosive effect on your faith. Rather, they can be the open door the Holy Spirit uses to enter your life, open your eyes to greater truths about God, and draw you closer to Jesus.

**Does the concept of "believing doubt" make sense
to you? Where do you see it in your life?**

In your struggles with doubt, have you found that they lead you more toward faith or away from it? Why?

What changes do you need to make in your attitude or your prayers to adjust the trajectory of your doubts? What do you need to confess or repent of? What do you need to pray "help my unbelief" over?

In what areas of life is pride or self-sufficiency holding you back and feeding your doubts or struggles?

How have you seen doubts draw you into deeper faith in Jesus? If they haven't, what specific prayers can you pray, so the trajectory of your doubts becomes faith-building instead of damaging?

What aspect of this study has challenged you the most? What has encouraged you most?

Leader Guide

Prepare for each group session with prayer. Ask the Holy Spirit to work through you and the group discussion as you point to Jesus each week through God's Word.

REVIEW the personal studies and the group sessions ahead of time.

PRAY for each person in the group.

CREATE A COMFORTABLE ENVIRONMENT. If group members are uncomfortable, they'll be distracted and therefore not engaged in the group experience.

INCLUDE OTHERS. Your goal is to foster a community in which people are welcome just as they are, but are encouraged to grow spiritually. Always be aware of opportunities to include anyone who visits the group and invite new people to join your group.

NO ONE DOMINATES—NOT EVEN THE LEADER. Be sure your time speaking as a leader takes up less than half your time together as a group. Politely guide the discussion if anyone dominates.

GOD AND HIS WORD ARE CENTRAL. Opinions and experiences can be helpful, but God has given us the truth. Trust Scripture to be the authority and God's Spirit to work in people's lives. You can't change anyone, but God can. Continually point people to the Word and to active steps of faith.

Session 1

This session is primarily about the nature of doubt and how people encounter it. It doesn't seek to address particular apologetic or personal questions people are struggling with. Some answers will come in the sessions to follow, but primarily this study aims to frame doubt and our response to it so people can handle it well rather than seeking to answer all their questions. Your goal as the leader is not to be the "answer person" but to help group members understand a framework of who God is, who we are, and how our doubts and questions fit in that.

KEY TAKEAWAYS

- Doubt is, at its base, simply not knowing. Therefore, doubt is not necessarily a sin.

- Doubt is common to everyone because of human limitations, sin nature, and God's infinity and holiness.

- Just because we don't understand something about God doesn't make it untrue or not good (See Psalm 139).

- The question isn't whether we doubt, but how we doubt, and that will be addressed in coming weeks.

DO's & DON'Ts

DO facilitate discussion about the nature of doubt and where it comes from.
DO emphasize the holiness and greatness of God and how that's expansive, infinite, and mysterious to us.
DO emphasize what scripture says about the nature and character of God and point out the ways we can know God and why we can trust Him.
DO be comfortable with tension and willing to work through discussion with some tension and lack of clear resolution.
DO always come back to the authority of Scripture as God's revelation of Himself.

DON'T focus on individual doubts or questions people may bring up. These will be distractions and make one person's experience paramount.
DON'T turn this into an apologetic study seeking to prove or give evidence for any particular argument.
DON'T feel the need to solve people's doubts or give neat, tidy answers to complex questions.

PRAY FOR

- Clarity of mind and humility of spirit.

- Honesty among group members so real struggles are brought before God.

- Scripture to be clear and speak into hearts.

- Eyes to see what God says about Himself and hearts to receive even complicated, difficult truths.

Session 2

This session doesn't offer much in the way of good news. It mostly sets up the dark background of unbelief against which the light of Christ will shine in the coming sessions. That's OK and on purpose. It's good to raise tough questions and make tough statements to get under people's skin. Their discomfort and desire for answers will, hopefully, open them up to the good news to come. But for now, let things stay somber.

Try not to let this session become an exercise in thinking about doubt abstractly. Think about it personally. Lead group members to consider their experiences with doubt and questions. And remember that if you have struggled or dealt with doubt, so too have others in your group, so be gracious. We're all approaching these big questions about God from a place of need.

KEY TAKEAWAYS

- Hebrews 11:1 deals in tension; faith and doubt are inextricably linked. There can be doubt without faith but no faith without doubt.

- Unbelieving doubt isn't simply struggling to believe or know something; it's an unwillingness to believe. This is when doubt becomes sin.

- To have unbelieving doubt is to be a practical atheist; there's no real difference between believing there's no God and "believing" in a God you won't trust.

- Unbelieving doubt is foolish, the way of destruction. The fear of the Lord is the beginning of wisdom and also the basis for faith.

DO's & DON'Ts

DO let this session stay somber.

DO encourage group members to examine their own hearts, motives, beliefs, attitudes, and struggles honestly.

DO tie back to session one and the infinite greatness of God, especially when discussing fear of the Lord.

DO help group members see the cost of doubt over time and how it erodes faith.

DON'T feel the need to jump to a happy ending or give quick answers to hard questions.

DON'T condemn or come down hard on doubters. They need hope, not the hammer.

PRAY FOR

- Conviction of unbelief.

- Honesty among group members so real struggles are brought before God.

- Wisdom, as in fear of the Lord and genuine belief in Him.

- Willingness to press on through difficult topics, doubts, or conversations.

Session 3

Adam and Eve wanted to be their own gods rather than following God, and their doubts were what the Bible calls "foolishness"—the way of destruction. All doubts that we allow to pull us away from trusting God inevitably lead to destruction. But there is a better way, a way in which our doubts can be a catalyst for greater faith.

That's where we're going in the remainder of this study. It's imperative that we know how not to respond to doubts; it protects us. But it doesn't lead us to a more vibrant life in Christ and stronger faith, and that's where we want to go as followers of Jesus. We'll look at a story of a doubting man's interaction with Jesus from a few different angles to see what we can learn about how we should respond to doubts and how Jesus responds to us.

KEY TAKEAWAYS

- We're rarely if ever, inclined to bring doubts to Jesus.

- We are always inclined to find another solution or distraction than Jesus.

- The father in this story wasn't a perfect man; he was a man who acted in faith despite many obstacles to doing so.

- Jesus is the helper. Our actions don't resolve doubts; they simply direct doubts to the one who has the power to resolve and help.

DO's & DON'Ts

DO help group members reflect on what it means to "take doubts to Jesus."
DO consider real actions and habits group members can take to respond well to their doubts.
DO reflect on the real hardships the father faced, the real evil and pain in his life, so that the story carries weight with group members.
DO connect this session with the earlier sessions, especially as it pertains to the infinity and character of God.

DON'T make the father the hero of the story. He's an example of faith, and Jesus is the hero.
DON'T settle for easy or pat answers to questions about what we can do with our doubts. Dig for specifics, for the kinds of answers that reflect a direction change.
DON'T make it sound like the entirety of overcoming doubts rests on how people act. Remember, the point is they're bringing their doubts to Jesus for help.

PRAY FOR

- Open eyes to where and how we've relied on self instead of on Jesus.

- Open hearts to Jesus, especially for those tied up in fear or shame.

- Willingness to discuss and admit real doubts, real fears, real struggles so they can be brought into the light of Christ and His Word.

Session 4

In this session, we want to be open and clear with God as we wrestle with doubts and trials. We want to be humble before God and one another, as the father was. We want to be seekers, looking for what truth and hope God has for us. Let this be our attitude and aim as we discuss this text with one another and see what it has to teach us.

KEY TAKEAWAYS

- The tone and attitude of the father toward Jesus are exemplifications of faith.

- "I believe; help my unbelief" is not just a prayer; it's a paradigm of handling the tensions and struggles of faith and doubt.

- This prayer is applicable to those in your group who are in a solid place of faith and those who are struggling deeply with matters of faith.

DO's & DON'Ts

DO be reflective, not just explanatory or expositional.

DO pray this prayer for yourselves and with your group.

DO ask direct questions about what group members believe that bolsters their faith.

DO ask direct questions about what group members struggle to believe that they need help with.

DO remind and encourage the group that this prayer is an ongoing thing, to be leaned on throughout all of life.

DON'T hide your own struggles with doubt and belief.

DON'T use this prayer as a faith "band-aid" to be slapped on any difficult question.

DON'T crush the strugglers in your group for their "help my unbelief" moments and realities.

DON'T let the "good Christians" in your group off the hook, but rather dig into what "help my unbelief" means for them.

PRAY FOR

- Understanding of the depth and richness of this simple sentence as a framework for growing in faith throughout all of life, no matter the situation or circumstance.

- Group members who are struggling deeply with doubts, that this prayer would give them peace and freedom.

- Group members who aren't struggling and think they're OK, that they would see where they need the Spirit's help with their unbelief.

Session 5

In the last two sessions, we focused on faith. The father is an example of faith for us. This is why it made sense to focus on his actions, his attitude, and his words.

But by focusing so much on him, we ran the risk of doing what journalists are told never to do: bury the lede. To bury the lede is to overlook the most important point of a story. In this case, it would also mean to overlook the main character. The father in this story is relatable and pivotal, but he's not the hero. Jesus is. This session focuses on Him.

KEY TAKEAWAYS

- Jesus loves doubters.

- Jesus accepts anyone who comes to Him humbly.

- Jesus won't let you wallow in doubt.

- Jesus will always give you what you need but not always what you want.

DO's & DON'Ts

DO Invite. This is the clearest opportunity in this study for someone to meet Jesus for the first time.

DO be patient with those who struggle with the idea that God gives pains and thorns. That's a difficult idea.

DO emphasize hope. Jesus' response to doubters is the best thing for us.

DON'T let people think Jesus welcomes us no matter our attitude. Humility and dependence are what He is looking for.

DON'T make excuses where God doesn't. Paul says God gave him the thorn, so we don't need to be shy about saying the same.

DON'T feel pressure to clarify things that are in God's wisdom and are beyond you. Faith and the Holy Spirit have got your back.

PRAY FOR

- Recognition that Jesus LOVES doubters.

- Openness to Jesus' correction to our doubts and questions.

- Willingness to accept how Jesus meets our needs as best for our present and future.

Session 6

The goal of our time together in this group has been to find greater freedom—freedom in Christ and the knowledge that He accepts and loves strugglers and doubters. Hope that your doubts aren't what defines you, nor will they condemn you if you bring them to Jesus. Jesus is beyond our capacity to consider or imagine, and He's present and personal, inviting you to Himself. And that is why we can hope even in the midst of doubts.

KEY TAKEAWAYS

- God can use doubt to lead us to faith.

- God gives faith; we don't create it in ourselves.

- Questions and doubts can be an open door for the Holy Spirit to work if we bring them in humility.

- Humility comes from staring deeply into God's word and gaining a right understanding of Him and ourselves.

DO's & DON'Ts

DO trace the entire study to this point so group members can see how all the ideas fit together

DO ask how people have changed, grown, or been helped by the study.

DO focus on the greatness and wonder of God.

DO leave people with hope—Jesus welcoming doubters and the Holy Spirit working through their struggles

DON'T be frustrated if people (or you) still struggle. This study isn't a magic pill.

DON'T forget to always point back to scripture and to God as the resolution to doubts.

DON'T lead people to believe that scripture will answer every question

PRAY FOR

• Humility within the group so that people will come to the Bible with open hearts and the Spirit can work in them.

• Comfort and peace for the struggling.

• A strengthened foundation of faith so you and the group can respond better to doubts in the future.

• A clearer understanding of God's works, His character, and His promises.

WHAT HAPPENS WHEN YOU SEE EVERYTHING IN THE LIGHT OF THE GOSPEL?

It's that moment when you realize your heart cannot begin to hold all the love Jesus has for you. When you realize that moralism is empty and all of life is really about His life, death, and resurrection.

This Bible study series will lead you on a one-year journey through the entire storyline of Scripture, showing how Jesus is the Hero from beginning to end.

When the light of the gospel transforms just one individual, it has the power to illuminate your group, your church, and even your entire community.

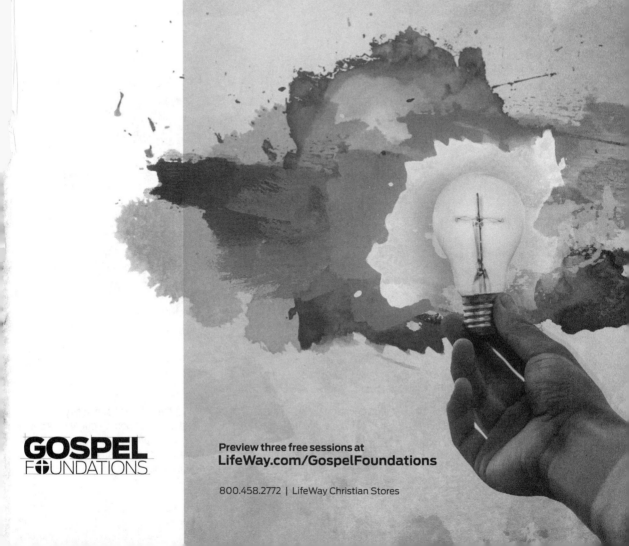

WHERE TO GO FROM HERE

We hope you were challenged and inspired by *Help My Unbelief*. Now that you've completed this study, here are a few possible directions you can go for your next one. See more at LifeWay.com/BalancedDiscipleship

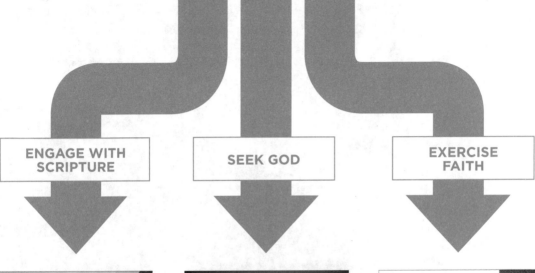

ENGAGE WITH SCRIPTURE

SEEK GOD

EXERCISE FAITH

Understand that works don't save us, rather good works follow true faith as our beliefs and actions line up with each other. (13 sessions)

Learn how to read the various types of biblical literature in a way that unlocks God's intended meaning. (9 sessions)

Get off the sidelines of ministry and let Jesus work through you as you pray, go, and give of yourself to make an eternal difference. (6 sessions)